CHINA

Shanghai has grown more rapidly in recent decades than almost any other city on the planet. The Bund, the waterfront embankment of the original old city, looks across to the skyscrapers in Pudong.

Hunan Province boasts the marvellous karst landscape of Wulingyuan. Over 3,000 sandstone pillars and mountains are interlaced with rivers, waterfalls, lakes, caves and two huge natural bridges.

ABOUT THIS BOOK

Repression and revolutions, major inventions in the past and unparalleled economic growth today are keywords summing up thousands of years of Chinese history. What began 4,000 years ago as a small kingdom was divided into many small dynastic principalities, was re-united and ultimately became a world power. The monarchy was not brought down until the revolution that began in 1911 and the founding of the People's Republic in 1949 marked the birth of modern China.

China has never been simply a country but rather a special world apart; it was always "everything between the four seas". The Chinese emperors, the "Sons of Heaven", believed that for millennia until the British army appeared off Canton in the 19th century, forced open the Chinese markets and encouraged the start of the opium trade. Two thousand years before, when no one in Europe had even thought about such things, the first kites were being constructed, some 600 years after the first book was printed here. Moreover, this is the land that invented playing cards, paper money and fireworks. China has undergone more dramatic changes in its long history than any other country. The flourishing modern Chinese economy continues to amaze the rest of the world. Despite all the upheavals that have swept through the land, the Chinese people have clung to their Confucian and Buddhist traditions.

What makes this country so enthralling is the bright mosaic of its landscapes, people and cultures. The world's third largest nation is home to about a billion Han Chinese as well as numerous ethnic minorities, including Thai peoples, Tibetans, Turkmen and Mongolians living in what are officially designated "autonomous regions". Each of these ethnic groups have developed art, customs and traditions of their own, which add an incredible richness and diversity to the intricately wrought tapestry of Chinese culture. What all ethnic groups have in common, however, are the use of the Chinese characters, which is taught at all schools and is read throughout China.

This extraordinary country will be presented in this illustrated guide in an entirely different way. First, we will show you the breathtaking diversity of China in geographically arranged chapters. The following atlas section facilitates finding sights you want to see and places you'd like to visit. Moreover, it includes lots of invaluable tips for tourism. At the end, an index linking the picture and the atlas sections contains the internet addresses of the most important sights as a convenient aid to finding out more about them. All this is to help you to discover China, a land that straddles tradition and modernity.

The Publisher

A girl poses by Tian Tan, the Temple of Heaven in Beijing. On the right in the background, a part of the showpiece of the grounds can be seen, the Hall of Harvest Prayer with its three-tiered roof.

CONTENTS

China is the world's most populous country, with a population of 1.3 billion. Twenty-two provinces and five autonomous regions as well as the Special Administrative Regions of Hong Kong and Macau unite in a vast diversity of landscapes, peoples and traditions. It extends from Siberian Heilongjiang in the north to tropical Hainan in the south, from sparsely settled Sinkiang in the west to densely populated Zhejiang in the east.

Far in the north-east of China, the rising sun and the clouds lying low between the peaks of the Great Chimgan Mountains and create an impressive backdrop (small picture). In the province of Chilin on the border to North Korea, framed by the precipitous snow-covered mountains of the Chiangbai massif, lies Lake Tianchi, the "Lake of Heaven," which at some points is up to 200 m (219 yds) deep.

NORTH-EASTERN CHINA

Bounded on the west by Mongolia, on the north by Russia and in the east by North Korea, north-east China stretches between the grasslands of Inner Mongolia, the birch forests of Siberia and the mountains edging Korea. The region has been fought over down through the centuries: Genghis Khan swept through it, the Russians wanted to extend the empire southwards to ice-free seas and the Japanese established the puppet state of Manchukuo there in 1932. For most of the time, however, this region has remained part of China.

Family life among Mongolian nomads is lived out entirely in the traditional portable felt dwellings called yurts. Below: Inner Mongolia is a hilly, green steppe stretching in all directions as far as the eye can see. Mongolians love celebrating riotous festivals and erect large yurts, that they decorate with bright banners, for these joyous occasions. Above: The Hulun Buir Shadi region is located in Inner Mongolia, where nomadic tribes still collect their herds to bring them home at dusk.

The Chimgan Mountains and Hulun Buir Shadi

Big and Little Chimgan are ridges separating China from Siberia and Mongolia. They represent one of China's largest forested regions and most towns look like logging camps. Very few people live here because the climate is harsh in winter and hot in summer. The Argun, a source of the river Amur that for centuries was the hotly contested border between Russia and China, rises in this area. In the west, the range slopes down towards Inner Mongolia and the lush grasslands and pasturage of Hulun Buir Shadi. This is the land of the yurts with their conical tops. Even before the days of Genghis Khan, they housed the nomads and were the focus of their lives. The Chinese government has only succeeded to a limited extent in its efforts to make the nomads sedentary. They have retained their unique customs and are to this day superb riders and wrestlers.

The Siberian Tiger is the largest and most powerful of all the big cats, including the majestic lion. When stalking prey, the Siberian tiger is both hunter and hunted. It kills wild boar, deer, cattle and mules but is itself a much coveted hunting trophy. A shy, nocturnal animal, it is usually solitary. Today, the ancient birch forests and mountains of the northeast Chinese province of Jilin are the Siberian Tiger's habitat. In summer, its coat is short and smooth, like that of tigers in tropical regions. In winter, however, it grows particularly thick and long.

THE SIBERIAN TIGER

Only about twenty to thirty Siberian Tigers still live in the wild in northern China, on the Russian border, scattered along the Amur and its tributaries. Although the Siberian Tiger is a protected species, it is acutely threatened with extinction from being hunted. One of the main reasons for this sorry state of affairs is that the Siberi-an Tiger is of great interest to practitioners of East Asian medicine. The animal represents lucrative booty for hunters because there is virtually no part of its body that is not used in this form of medicine. Its hide, bones, teeth, claws, blood, even gallstones and genitals are believed to be efficacious remedies for such widely ranging health problems such as rheumatism, epilepsy, bad skin and weak eyesight. Certain substances in the Siberian Tiger are supposed to enhance human intelligence and make men more potent. However, it is not just in China that tiger medicine is in such demand; it also commands high prices in the US and Europe. Moreover, sumptuous Siberian Tiger fur coats bring broad export profit margins. In Chinese astrology, the virtues of courage and independence are ascribed to a man born under the sign of the tiger. He is said to grab the limelight but to be equally willing to make sacrifices. The "Tiger woman" is characterized as intelligent and sincere.

The Harbin International Ice and Snow Festival ("Lantern Festival") takes place in Harbin every year in January and February. Large ice sculptures are set up in Zhaolin Garden. Cut from the Songhua River, blocks of ice are turned by local artists and specialists from abroad into animals, mythical figures and wonders of architecture. Such celebrated sights as the Great Wall of China, the Arc de Triomphe in Paris and the Pyramids at Giza are recreated in ice. The sculptures are impressive at night as they are illuminated from within by bright neon lighting.

Harbin

Harbin, China's most northerly provincial capital, was originally a small fishing village that became a junction of the Chinese Eastern Railway when the Russians were building it as an extension of the Trans-Siberian Railway. Churches with onion domes and villas in the older sections of the city recall that era. After the Russo-Japanese war in 1904 to 1905, Harbin was ceded to Japan and was made the capital of the puppet state of Manchukuo, with Puyi, the last Chinese emperor, as ruler. After the October Revolution, Russian emigrants poured into Harbin seeking asylum. Dubbed the Paris of the East and the Oriental St Petersburg, the modern city has developed into a thriving industrial center boasting several universities. The most important annual event is the Harbin International Ice and Snow Festival, when a Disneyland of ice sculptures recreate the world's greatest monuments.

Dense forest covers more than 200,000 ha (772 sq miles) around the Changbai Mountains. This region is home to more than eighty-three species, both broadleaf and conifer, including the Korean Pine. The area became known because the Ginseng plant grows here. Above: Some of the sixteen peaks encircling Lake Tianchi in the Changbai Mountains. Right-hand page: at an altitude of more than 2,000 m (2,187 yds) above sea level, the lake is frozen over from September to June although hot springs keep it free of ice during those months.

The Changbai Mountains

Changbai Shan means "Everwhite Mountain". For the most part snow-capped, this mountain range runs between north-eastern China and North Korea. It is China's largest biosphere reserve and the habitat of rare flora, including certain therapeutic herbs, and fauna, such as Manchurian Tigers and Snow Leopards. The most famous peak is the 2,744-m-high (9,002 ft) Baekdu Shan, the "White-headed Mountain", a volcano that is now always frozen and has not been active for some 300 years. Its vast crater filled with water over the many years to form Tianchi, "Heavenly Lake". The inhabitants of this region look on the lake as a divine gift, which only "the fortunate" are able to see. Its waters are almost invariably mirror-smooth, the lake is crystal clear and, when the weather is fine, it reflects the grotesque volcanic rock formations looming over it.

The grounds of the Imperial Palace of Shenyang, the only existing royal palace in China outside of Beijing, sprawl over an area of 60,000 sq m (64,5600 sq ft). In the hall of the Exalted Rulers, Chongzheng Dian, the emperor's throne can be seen (left above and center). In the eastern part of the complex stands the oldest of the palace buildings, the octagonal Hall of the Great Rulers, Dazheng Dian (left below). The walls of these buildings are rich with embellished reliefs such as this golden dragon (large picture). Above: A group of Court officials with the Chinese emperor.

Shenyang

Shenyang (Shengjing: population over five million) is now the capital of the north Chinese province of Liaoning, which is one of the largest major industrial centers in China. Transnational and domestic car manufacturers as well as mechanical and electronic engineering companies have branches here. In the 17th century, the city, which was then called Mukden, was for some years the seat of the Manchurian Qing emperors. Eager to compete with the Forbidden City in Peking, they added room after room to Mukden Palace until it boasted a grand total of more than 300 rooms and halls. Even after the seat of government was moved to Peking in 1644, the emperors would return regularly for hunting and visiting the tombs of their ancestors. For years, the Palace has been a museum boasting great treasures of Chinese art from various periods.

The Gate of Heavenly Peace with its portrait of Mao Tse Tung stands on the square of the same name on one of the main traffic routes through the lively center of Beijing. Large picture: A view of the north- eastern tower and the around 50 m (55 yds) wide moat that surrounds the Forbidden City in Beijing. Wall, towers and the gate of the imperial Palace are reflected in the smooth surface of the water.

NORTHERN CHINA

Northern China extends along both sides of the old Silk Road, from the quiet grassy hills of Inner Mongolia across the Great Wall to Beijing, the capital, and along the Yellow River to the Mogao Grottoes of Dunhuang. The region encompasses fertile plains in the east, verdant meadows in the north, deserts in the west and densely populated areas in the south. Four millennia of Chinese history live on here. The north is the cradle of Chinese civilization; chinese culture is rooted here, where Chinese customs and observances originated.

Large picture: The north side of the Forbidden City with the Gate of the Divine Might. Left from above: the entrance to the Hall of Supreme Harmony, the handle of a water jar, the new Dragon wall and one of the four corner towers. Above: The Gate of Supreme Harmony. Right-hand page: Lions of Fo as Guardians of the Gate, a side gateway to the Inner City, a lion's head and the Gate of Earthly Tranquillity.

Beijing and the Forbidden City

The vast Chinese empire was ruled from the Forbidden City for nearly four centuries until republican opposition movements put paid to the monarchy in 1911. The last emperor was forced to leave his palace in 1924. Only then was the public granted access to the Palace, which had previously been reserved for the emperor, his wives and concubines and a large number of eunuchs. Apart from the imperial family, only ministers and officials of the highest rank were admitted to audiences and important events. The rectangular structure with halls for official occasions and separate, inaccessible living quarters for the imperial family, is surrounded by a broad moat and a high wall with four massive towers. The Forbidden City is now a museum with magnificent halls, bright decorated dwellings and a treasure-trove of great Chinese art objects.

On a terraced base in the grounds of the Temple of Heaven stands the Hall of Harvest Prayer with its three-tiered roof. Above: The Hall of Harvest Prayer and the Hall of the Vault of Heaven from different perspectives. Right below: The interior and vaulting of the Hall of Harvest Prayer.

Beijing and the Temple of Heaven

Throughout Chinese history, sacrificial rites were the most important of the ruler's official duties. To preserve harmony and order on earth, the emperor celebrated the winter solstice each year in the Temple of Heaven in Beijing. The Temple was the symbol of his spiritual and temporal powers, of heaven and earth. The architecture radiates this sense of order: the northern, semicircular part symbolizes heaven, the southern, square element, the earth. To perform the ritual, the emperor would go, accompanied by a magnificent procession, to the Temple precincts. After fasting for three days, he would proceed to the Temple of the Vault of Heaven to meditate and finally to the Altar of Heaven to make sacrifice. The altar stands on three white marble terraces. The stones on the surfaces are arranged as multiples of nine, which was the celestial number.

The art of theatrical make-up and cosmetics looks back on a long, highly diverse tradition in Chinese drama (large picture). Towards the close of the 18th century, an entirely new style of opera production developed: Peking opera. The bright face painting became a quintessential part of performance and characterization; the various characters in the cast are still defined by their make-up. In Peking opera, male and female leads of noble character tend to be quite naturally made up while the faces of villains are disguised behind bizarre cosmetic masks.

PEKING OPERA

Peking opera is the form of Chinese drama best known outside China. Although the pitch and timbre of the singing voices and musical accompaniment may occasionally sound strange to unschooled Western ears, Peking opera represents a significant expression of Chinese culture as reflected in the sophisticated make-up on the actors' faces and their showy costumes embroidered in lovely tones contrasting with the simplicity of the props. The performers, often singer, actor and acrobat in one, take years learning and rehearsing their parts. Peking opera unites music, singing, dance, pantomime and acrobatics in a complex system of signs. The content of the pieces performed is based on historical fact, ancient legends or literature. Wooden rhythm instruments point a performance in four general directions: a slow beat stands for contemplation, a medium one underscores narrative, a fast beat signalizes pleasure and excitement and a mixed beat is used for the entre'acts. There is scarcely any scenery since the actors' pantomime and gestures explain what is going on to the audience. The shades of the faces and costumes characterize the cast by type: red stands for a good character, black for decency, white is the code for deceitfulness and cruelty, yellow symbolizes brutality and blue courage.

The Zhichun Pavilion stands on an island in Kunming Lake. Above: the Marble Boat pavilion, the Tower of Buddhist Fragrance and one of the elegant bridges. Below: a pavilion on the lake reached by the Long Corridor and the arch of the Jade Belt Bridge, an 18th-century Moon bridge.

THE YELLOW RIVER

In the course of the years, dams have broken causing disastrous flooding and the lower reaches of the Huang He, the "Yellow River", have often changed course to flow in new beds to the Yellow Sea. From its source in the Kunlun Mountains in the high plateau of Tibet, the Yellow River flows through many gorges to Lanzhou, crosses the Great Wall of China, meets up with it again to cut through a loess plateau and reaches broad lowlands before flowing into the sea through a broad delta. The Huang He and the Yangtze River are the two great historic Chinese rivers. The ancestors of the present-day Chinese followed the course of the Yellow River, which made the land arable, and its valley was the fertile soil on which grew ancient and medieval China. After the terrible floods of 1855, the Yellow River was forced to flow between embankments that were 10 m (11 yds) high but this measure did not prevent flooding. Today, only about a third of its volume of water reaches the delta since water being drawn off for drinking water, industrial use and agricultural irrigation causes parts of the riverbed to dry up during the summer months. Many stretches of the Yellow River are not navigable because the water level fluctuates so widely during a given year. The Grand Canal links it with the Yangtze River and Beijing.

Mount Hua, Hua Shan (2,200 m/ 7,218 ft) is often veiled in mist. Above: The Yunnan Stub-nosed Monkey, the Takin and the Golden Snub-nosed Monkey are endemic to the region. Right-hand page: The western peak is one of the highest of the five in this range.

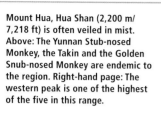

Hua Shan

Hua Shan, Mount Hua, at sunset is one of the most beautiful sights in the mountains of China. The five peaks of this range together comprise one of the Five Sacred Mountains of Taoism, which are also named after the five cardinal directions of Chinese geomancy and are scattered about China. Lao Tse is said to have spent some time at the Taoist temples on the southern peak of Hua Shan. On the western peak, the "Splendid Mountain", stands a temple consecrated to the Three Pure Ones of Taoism. The central peak is called the Mountain of the Jade Pure. Many Chinese emperors came here to commemorate their ancestors. These peaks, all of them over 2,000 m (76,562 ft) high, still draw thousands of tourists from China and abroad who are fascinated by the sacredness and beauty of this range. Hua Shan is located about 120 km (74 miles) east of Xi'an.

Over 7,000 lifesize terracotta soldiers, some accompanied by their steeds, have been excavated in Lintong, near the city of Xi´an. They guard the tomb of the first emperor of a united China, Qin Shihuangdi. Above: The Great Wild Goose Pagoda is located about 4 km (2 miles) from Xi´an. It was built in the seventh century to house valuable Buddhist writings and Buddha statues. Right-hand page: The quality of this staggering find as art has made the Terracotta Army world-famous. Light fades the shades of the doughty polychrome warriors.

Xi´an and the Terracotta Army

A farmer digging a well near Xi´an in 1974, brought to light a lifesize terracotta figure. This discovery ushered in one of the greatest archaeological finds of the 20th century, a terracotta standing army of nearly 8,000 helmeted and armed warriors and horses dating from the third century BC. At that time, Qin Shihuangdi united China and became its first important emperor. He was buried in a tomb guarded by the Terracotta Army not far from Xi´an, formerly Chang´an, one of the four great ancient capitals of the country. Hundreds of archaeologists are still coming up with treasures that beggar belief. Surrounded by a wall with massive towers, the city boasts interesting monuments from its heyday, such as the Drum Tower and the Bell Tower. The Great Wild Goose Pagoda, 64 m (70 yds) high, is located outside town. Today, Xi´an is a big industrial city and a tourist magnet.

Haibao Pagoda in Yinchuan boasts eleven tiers of eaves. Above: The triangle of 108 pagodas. Below: A street in Yinchuan. Bottom from left: Dunes in the Tengeli Desert, the Sand Lake north of Yinchuan, the Xi Xia dynasty mausoleum pyramid and the Linggui towers from the Tang dynasty.

Yinchuan, Helan Shan and Xi Xia Wangling

As legend has it, Yinchuan was founded by the Feng-huang, the Chinese phoenix, who spotted the jade-green land in the midst of the desert. Yinchuan is situated on a high plateau at the foot of the Helan Mountains, through which the Yellow River runs from the south-west. Here, Nomadic peoples immortalized themselves nearly 3,000 years ago with rock drawings and engravings. Nanguan Mosque with its five domes and the old Drum Tower at the center are old-city landmarks. Xi Xia Wangling is 30 km (19 miles) from Yinchuan. There, the emperors of the Western Xia dynasty, who were originally Tangut tribesmen, a Qiangic-Tibetan people, were buried with their families in stone pyramids. A triangle of 108 pagodas in twelve rows stands on the west bank of the Yellow River. These are lamaistic dagobas, believed to be China's oldest cluster of Buddhist towers.

The 35-m-long (38 yds) statue in the Great Buddha Temple at Zhangye. Below: The temple entrance. Above: Jiayuguan Fortress in Gansu. Right below: Bactrian camels in the Gobi, Bayanzag fossil site, and the tomb of the Honghua Princess.

Gobi Desert, Jiayuguan, Zhangye and Wuwei

The Gobi is a cold desert of incredible diversity: drift-sand, mountains, salt lakes, steppe, semi-desert, forests and a wealth of fauna. Famously, the first petrified dinosaur eggs were found in the Gobi and the nucleus of Genghis Khan's empire was here. The first modern Chinese rockets were launched into space from the Gobi. Jiayuguan is on the fringes of the Gobi, marking the pass where the Great Wall of China ends and can be entered. The massive fortress guards the pass. Jiayuguan City is located on the old Silk Road, a last rest stop for traders and tourists. The city of Zhangye, south-east of Jiayuguan, was an important base for merchant caravans. Marco Polo was sure to have seen China's biggest reclining Buddha here. To the east is Wuwei on the Silk Road, where the famous "Galloping Bronze Horse" of Gansu was found.

About 25 km (15 miles) south-east of the city of Dunhuang are the Mogao Grottoes, also known as Caves of the Thousand Buddhas. Here, in the close to 500 caves are thousands of frescos and more than 2,000 statues, including this gigantic Buddha. Above: One of the five monasteries built to protect the Grottoes. Right-hand page below: A view of Dunhuang and Crescent Lake.

Dunhuang and the Mogao Grottoes

The Buddhist cave temples of Mogao near the oasis city of Dunhuang, where the Silk Road forks before the vast Taklaman Desert, are among China's most celebrated historic monuments. The story of what was once more than 1,000 grottoes began in the fourth century with a simple monk retreating into the mountains to meditate. Of those grottoes, also known as the Caves of the Thousand Buddhas, 492 have survived. This testimonial to a Buddhist past with its invaluable paintings and statues symbolizes the rich cultural diversity of the Silk Road at its eastern extremity. A hoard of ancient manuscripts, paintings on silk and wood-carvings was found in one of the grottoes. These finds make the grottoes the most important source for the history of Buddhism in China. To protect the originals, copies of the paintings and sculptures have been made for display.

Above: Sailing boats glide in the evening light over the South China Sea near Shantou, a port and industrial city on the east coast of Guangdong Province near the border with Fujian Province. Despite all the changes in the country, the tradition of early morning callisthenics on the Bund, the old Shanghai waterfront, is alive and kicking. Chinese do Tai Chi and Qi Gong in the morning hours (large picture).

EASTERN CHINA

Eastern China unites tradition, beautiful scenery, contemplative tranquillity and modernity: the industrial area around Shanghai, which records the world's highest economic growth is not far from remote monasteries, mountain wilderness as well as towns and villages thousands of years old. This is where Confucius was born, the sage whose teachings still shape China. The Grand Canal starts here, a 1,600-km-long (994 miles) waterway on which the emperors had rice, tea and silk shipped from south to north.

A bridge decorated with lanterns leads to the Confucian Temple in Nanjing (large picture). Above: The residence of Confucius' Kong family, with altar and his burial place in Qufu. Right below: Many statues throughout the land recognize the great Chinese scholars.

CONFUCIUS

Confucius (551–479 BC) was born into an impoverished aristocratic family in Qufu, the city in which he also died. It was not until long after his death that the sage was acclaimed in China as "the Teacher of Ten Thousand Generations". His teachings are neither a religion nor a real philosophy but rather a compilation of old observances and values. Today, they still influence broad sectors of public and private life in China. Confucian temples are still the most popular places for contemplation and thoughtful meditation. The Confucian principles governing ethics and politics are very simple to understand and follow. The sage called for brotherly love and compassion and respecting one's parents and family as well as loyalty to one's friends. Virtue, love, humanity and goodness are the pivotal concepts of the Confucian ethical doctrine, which is also applied to the state and public affairs. Confucianism requires neither belief in a higher power nor any form of mysticism; it is based on reason and ethics. According to Confucius, man is made for this life, to perfect it by his deeds. Personal conduct is based on observing the ancient laws that derive from ancestral tradition and are valid. Confucianism became, with Buddhism and Taoism, one of the "Three Ways" that have essentially shaped the lives and actions of the Chinese.

The Bund, the waterfront of historic Shanghai. Above: A dragon-head sculpture in the Yuyuan Gardens, the famous teahouse in the middle of a lake and Zhujiajiao, a river town near Shanghai. Right-hand page: The Feast of Lanterns and China's most famous shopping boulevard, Nanjing Lu.

The old center of Shanghai

By Chinese standards, Shanghai, which grew out of a small fishing village near the Yangtze River in the 19th century, is a very young city. The city's strategic location on a great river, its proximity to the sea and possession of one of the world's largest ports made Shanghai a major base for European and American international trade and commerce. Shanghai developed into two very different sections. On one side of the river, the Chinese side of Shanghai grew up in a tangle of narrow streets, markets, temples and crowded residential quarters; on the opposite bank, a cosmopolitan metropolis shaped by colonialism mushroomed, boasting banks, businesses and mansions on broad boulevards and the celebrated waterfront, the Bund. As an economic powerhouse, Shanghai has always rivalled Beijing, the political center of the country.

The modern architecture of the Shanghai Grand Theatre in downtown Shanghai is both Western and Asian in style. Above: The Bund, the old waterfront, looks across to towering new buildings in Pudong, where Shanghai's new finance and trade zone is located. Below: Bold solutions have been found for handling the volume of traffic pouring across the Huangpu River from old to new Shanghai. The large spheres of the Oriental Pearl Tower hold restaurants and observation platforms. The façade of the Shanghai Museum reflects modern Shanghai.

Modern Shanghai

For a good look at China's rise to a global economic giant and world player on the business stage, all you have to do is cross the Huangpu River to Pudong. Only a few years ago, farmers were still growing vegetables here and taking them to market in town. The old part of Shanghai across the river proved a stumbling-block to ambitious government plans for making Shanghai a second Hong Kong. Now, however, modern Shanghai glitters with dazzling contemporary architecture: the World Financial Center, the Grand Theatre, the Oriental Pearl Tower, the Jin Mao Tower, which is with 421 m (460 yds) the world's tallest hotel, and the Shanghai Museum, evoking an ancient bronze cauldron, which houses a superlative collection of Chinese art. A Transrapid magnetic levitation train links the new airport with downtown Shanghai.

Baoshi Pagoda on the West Lake in Hangzhou. Above: The Lake of Thousand Islands. Below: Buddha statues at Taihu Lake, a garden in Suzhou, the Grand Canal in Zhouzhuang and the Maitreya Buddha, Lingyin Temple. Right-hand page: View across the West Lake and a bridge in Hangzhou.

Wuxi, Suzhou, Hangzhou, Lake of Thousand Islands and Zhoushan

Wuxi is located on the Grand Canal, which shaped the city's destiny for seven centuries. From the many bridges, boats of all kinds can still be seen plying the canal as they have done for a thousand years. The Grand Canal between the Yangtze and Peking was one of the main supply lines and trade routes in imperial China. Suzhou, renowned for its canals, lovely gardens and fine temples, is also located on the Grand Canal. Hangzhou was once an imperial capital. The West Lake bordering on the city, dotted with little islands crowned with temples, draws large numbers of visitors. To the south-west is the enchanting crystal-clear Lake of Thousand Islands, a man-made body of water which was created by damming up the Qujiang (Qu River). The Zhoushan Archipelago at the southern end of the Yangtze delta has many ports serving the richest fishing grounds off the Chinese coast.

With bizarrely formed rocks and gnarled pines the Huangshan-Mountains fulfill the Chinese landscape ideal. Above: An archway in the village of Hongcun, typical dwellings and a traditional doorway in Xidi. Right-hand page: Cloud formations at Huangshan.

Huangshan and Xidi

"He who has seen the Huangshan once will never regret not having seen other mountains", runs a Chinese saying. The range, whose name means "Yellow Mountain", is one of the five most famous in China and has figured in painting and poetry since time immemorial. It has lost nothing of its fascination. Painters, poets and photographers still make annual pilgrimages to the Huangshan to gaze spellbound at the early morning spectacle of the rock formations emerging from the mist. At the foot of the Yellow Mountain is Xidi, a tiny, centuries-old village untouched by the ravages of time that has kept its Ming and Qing houses, its bright doors and roofs, its rural way of life and even its old water-supply system. One of the designated "Ancient Villages of Southern Anhui", Xidi is an open-air museum of the old Chinese settlement form and way of life.

A pilgrim path winds up Mount Wuyi. The valley below may be shrouded in mist while the peaks are gleaming in the sun. Above: One of numerous Taoist temples in the Mount Wuyi region in Fujian Province. Below: The tu lou, or round houses, in Yongding were built by individual families. An old man in a Mao jacket stands in front of one of these brick structures bearing the inscription "Long live Mao". The inner court enclosed in the concentric tiers of the various floors. Lanterns and garlands at the Spring Festival and a girl playing with a skipping rope.

Mount Wuyi and Yongding

In the seventh century, Mount Wuyi was at the heart of a small kingdom. Its rulers' palace still stands. Later, the mountains with their temples became an important Taoist center and ultimately the cradle of Neo-Confucianism. The red sandstone eastern range is steep and flat-topped. This region is renowned for the biodiversity of its Chinese rainforest with rare flora and fauna which are extinct elsewhere. Around AD 1000, the Hakka people fled down the Yellow River to southern Fujian Province, leaving famine and war behind them in north China. In Yongding, they built unique, fortress-like completely round clay-brick dwellings called tu lou, many of which rise several floors in multiple tiers enclosing a central round court. The kitchens and communal rooms are at ground level, provisions are stored on the first floor and above that are the living quarters.

Above: Dazu boasts thousands of statues and inscriptions revealing Taoist, Buddhist and Confucianist influences. Many of the grottoes hewn in the rock are over a thousand years old. The Lantern Festival is celebrated annually in Wuhan in February. Wave after wave of paper lanterns and large kites in animal shapes, each held securely by groups of people, swing through the streets.

CENTRAL CHINA

The heartland provinces of Henan, Hubei, Sichuan, Guizhou and Hunan are all south of the Huang He (Yellow River), clustered about the Yangtze. They share a continental climate: hot, humid summers and cool, rainy winters. This is the agricultural center of China. The countryside is densely populated with small villages and large cities, including the industrial city of Chongqing, Kaifeng, one of thE ancient capitals, Wuhan, the birthplace of the republican movement, and Changsha, the prime hub of the wheat trade.

Huge statues of Buddhist divinites stand in
the Longmen Grottoes at Luoyang. Below:
the ten-thousand Buddhas Cave is impressive.
Above: The Shaolin Monastery, famed for the
martial arts and Chan Buddhism practised
by its monks, is south-east of Luoyang: the
bright ceiling of the temple there, a monk
at prayers and a vivid dragon's head.

Kaifeng, Luoyang and Longmen

Medieval Kaifeng was called the world's largest city when it was the Song dynasty capital. Over a thousand monks lived in the more than sixty temples of this city on the Yellow River, that often rose above its banks to destroy large sections of Kaifeng. Today, the city is still a vibrant metropolis (population: over one million) with a celebrated ancient Jewish community once again numbering more than a thousand. Now, the capital of Henan Province, Luoyang, south of the Huang He, was the capital of China for centuries before Kaifeng enjoyed that status and is a pulsing industrial center. China's first Buddhist temple, the Temple of the White Horse, and the magnificent Longmen Grottoes, are only a few miles away. Thousands of Buddha statues, inscribed panels and forty-three pagodas are there to be visited. Unfortunately, some statues have sustained damage.

Extraordinarily narrow at Qutang, the Yangtze forms one of the celebrated Three Gorges at this point. Above: The Wu Xia Gorge, 40 km (25 miles) long, cuts through high mountains and is considered by many to be the most beautiful of the Three Gorges. Below: The undulating course of the Yangtze was dammed up at Sandouping near Yichang to form a vast reservoir. The world's biggest dam and manmade lake are to generate electricity and prevent flooding. Right-hand page: a traditional fishing boat against the magnificent backrop of the sheer gorge walls.

Yangtze

"The Long River" (Chang Jiang) is one of many Chinese names for the Yangtze, which rises in the Tibetan high plateau at an elevation of some 5,000 m (16,404 ft) to wind its way for 6,300 km (3,915 miles) to the China Sea near Shanghai. The Yangtze divides China into two climate zones, a cooler north and a warm south. The canal link with Peking was a major factor in making the Yangtze the country's main traffic artery. Even today, ocean-going ships can steam up the river for about 1,000 km (621 miles). The world's largest dam regulates the Yangtze where it flows through the Three Gorges – a reservoir 600 km (373 miles) long is formed here. The landscapes the great river glides through, past important cities such as Chongqing (Chungking), Wuhan, Nanjing (Nanking) and finally Shanghai, are some of the most beautiful in China.

This Buddha statue stands in one of the many grottoes near Dazu (large picture) which are now accepted as a Cultural World Heritage site. Amid the thousands and thousands of sculptures at Mount Baoding, 15 km (9 miles) to the north-east, the Tibetan Buddhist God of Death is pictured holding the Wheel of Life in his mouth (below right). The industrial city of Chongqing (Chungking) is located on a peninsula at the confluence of the Yangtze and the Jialing Rivers (above). Dozens of high-rise buildings shape the appearance of this modern Chinese city.

Chongqing and Dazu

Chongqing (Chungking) is surrounded on three sides by the Yangtze and the Jialing Rivers. A modern metropolis, it has a population of nearly four million. A steel manufacturing and ship-building center, Chongqing is located at the entrance to the Three Gorges of the Yangtze. The city has always been of strategic importance to China: in the Middle Ages, it was a Mongolian outpost, in the 19th century, a port used by Britain and Japan and in World War II it was the provisional capital of China and a base used by the American forces fighting against Japan. West of Chongqing, the Dazu Grottoes hold more than 60,000 Buddha statues that are so muniquely eclectic that they exemplify highly developed religious art. In 1999, they were declared a UNESCO Cultural World Heritage site on the grounds of their importance to the society, philosophy, religion and the traditional customs of China.

Tea and teahouses are an indispensable part of daily living in China. Enough kinds of tea are available: Jasmine tea, green tea, teas preferred in the West and teas mixed with blossoms and herbs (large picture). Canton is the capital of Guandong Province. Today a bustling modern metropolis, the city looks back on a long history as one of China's important centers of trade and commerce (above).

SOUTHERN CHINA

Southern China boasts enormously diverse scenery: enchanting mountain scenery, lush rice paddies, lovely beaches, humming modern cities. The climate is tropical. The sea and agriculture have shaped this part of China. The shopping centers in Hong Kong, bustling Canton, Macao, once a Portuguese colony and now known for its casinos, Guilin on the Li River and the tropical island of Hainan are just a few highlights of this region, whose inhabitants are entrepreneurial, friendly and connoisseurs of Chinese cuisine.

Extensive hillside terracing for rice cultivation in the mountains near Longsheng in northern Guangxi Zhuang. Rice fields were first laid out here more than 700 years ago. Above: Irrigation, the crop and gathering in the harvest. Right-hand page: A Hunan farmstead in flooded fields.

RICE CULTIVATION

"Had your rice today?" is a popular morning greeting in China. For most Chinese, a meal without rice is not eating at all. Archaeologists have shown that rice was cultivated very early in China. Rice cultivation was at first concentrated in the region around the Yangtze basin, where it shaped the local economy and culture. The me-thods of cultivating rice are as numerous as the species of rice available. Cultivating rice in the Chinese hill country is particularly laborious because it is often grown in such regions on steep hillside terraces that may look scenic but are extremely difficult to farm. After the monsoon, the rice field is carefully ploughed. Then the seedlings, which have been grown in seedbeds for about 40 days, are planted in the prepared rice field or paddy. Much of the work is labouriously done by hand. The vibrant green of the young rice plants is what makes terraced hillsides such lovely motifs in photography. The rice plants grow and ripen during the dry season and are har-vested after four or five months. Then the rice is taken to a rice mill or threshed by hand to separate the grains from the chaff. The hot, humid climate of inland China makes it possible to grow up to three rice crops a year. In China, rice is not just a staple food for man and beast; it is also important as a temple offering.

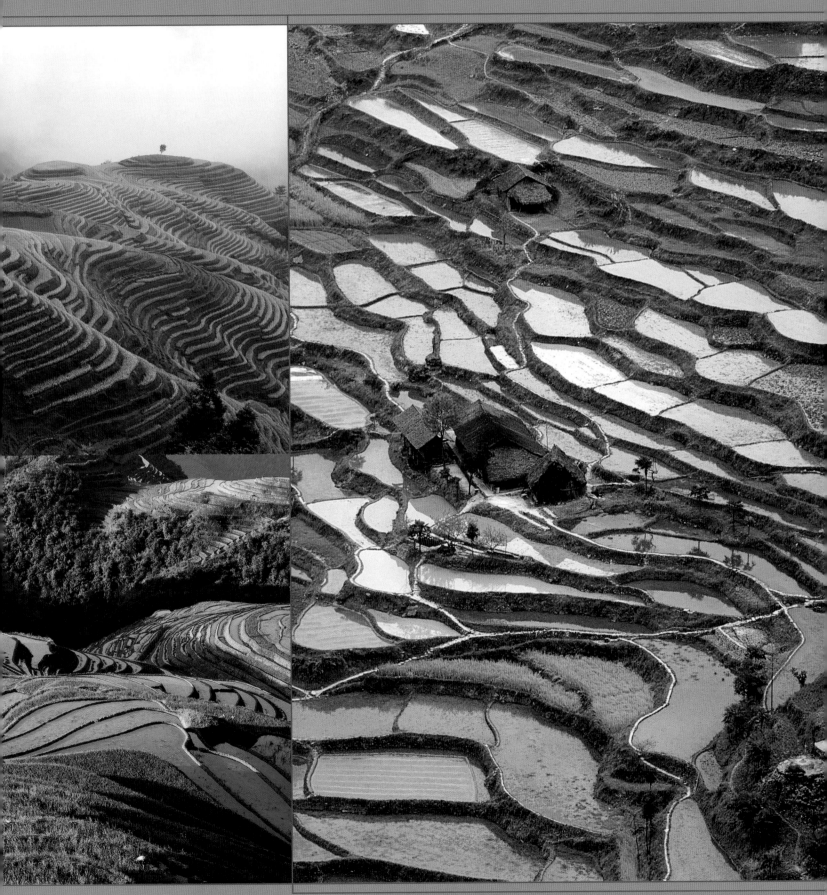

Virtually no tour of China would leave Guilin and the Li River off the itinerary. Its memorably romantic riverine landscape with its distinctive karst formations make Guilin one of the most extraordinary sights to see in China. Above: Guilin's scenery is celebrated by the Chinese them-selves as "best among all under heaven". At dawn or dusk, the river and mountains are particularly beautiful. Right-hand page: Fishermen using cormorants on bamboo rafts are typical of this landscape. Fish are attracted by lamp light and caught by the birds for the fishermen.

Guilin

Its marvellous location on the Li River, surrounded by steep limestone mountains overgrown with verdant vegetation, makes Guilin a high point of any trip to China. Its remoteness long consigned the city to obscurity as a garrison on the southern border of China. East of the city, Seven Star Park with its seven peaks alludes to the seven stars of the Great Bear constellation. The costumes and festivals of numerous ethnic minorities lend shades and vitality to Guilin cultural life. The main attractions for visitors are the hauntingly beautiful scenery along the river with its memorable rock formations and the ancient practice of fishing with trained cormorants. Fishermen use spotlights to lure their quarry to their bamboo rafts so it can be caught by cormorants. Each bird has a ring round its neck to keep it from swallowing the fish it so gracefully dives to catch.

From the shores of White Swan Lake, you can see Shamian Island, where the White Swan Hotel awaits discerning guests. A peaceful refuge from the frenetic pace of Guangzhou, the hotel looks out over the Pearl River. Above: A statue of the goddess of mercy and compassion over 40 m (44 yds) high and a hall with thousand figurines of the goddess stand on Lotus Mountain 45 km (28 miles) from Guangzhou. Below: The Garden Hotel and the Guangzhou International Hotel along with the Guangdong Olympic Stadium define the impressive Guangzhou skyline.

Guangzhou

The south China metropolis of Guangzhou (population nearly seven million) is on the Pearl River, only 200 km (124 miles) away from Hong Kong. It long vied as a trading post with the former British colony. Until 1918, the city was known abroad only as Canton. After the First Opium War (1834–1843), the English exerted political pressure on Canton to make it China's first free port and the transshipment point for opium from India. Modern Guangzhou is an important industrial center. The biannual Canton Fair is a trade fair showcasing global import and especially export commodities. The city boasts an array of luxury hotels, restaurants and bustling markets catering for businessmen and visitors. Guangzhou also has an elite university and some interesting sights to see, including the impressive Chen Family Ancestral Shrine and a richly endowed Western Han dynasty tomb.

View from the peak on the Kowloon Peninsula. Above: The Hong Kong Shanghai Bank headquarters is a Norman Foster building. Below: The seat of the Legislative Council with the Bank of China Tower. Next to it: Nathan Road in Tsim Sha Tsui on the Kowloon Peninsula.

Hong Kong

After 165 years as a British Crown Colony, Hong Kong became part of the People's Republic of China on July 1, 1997. The change in political status has had little effect on this vibrant hub of banking and services known for its lively stock exchange. One of Asia's most important ports, Hong Kong is still pivotal to global trade. An exhilarating city, Hong Kong boasts many outstanding restaurants, markets overflowing with produce, superlative shopping and a breathtaking backdrop of skyscrapers set between the mountains and the sea. Here, Chinese tradition and modern economic policy fuse. The people of Hong Kong are hardworking and entrepreneurial. Fabulous wealth rubs shoulders with appalling poverty. Probably one of the reasons why Hong Kong is still known as the "Gateway to China" is that it has remained a fascinating blend of East and West.

The Largo do Senado with its mosaic floor and fountains and many of the house fronts bring a breath of Lisbon to Macau. The city was a Portuguese colony until 1999. Above: The modern skyline and one of the floating casinos which have made Macau rich. Below: The A-Ma Temple and the bell of the Pau-Kong-Miu Pagoda.

Macao

A dash of Portugal, quite a bit of China and a lot of Las Vegas – that is Macau (Macao) today. When the Portuguese landed there in 1513, it was a fishing village in the Pearl River delta. A trade agreement concluded 40 years later made Macau the first European outpost in China, an entrepôt for the Portuguese silver and silk trade with the West. Another agreement, concluded in 1987, regulated the return of Macau to China in 1999. The old economic, social and legal system is to be retained during a transitional period while Macau, like Hong Kong, is a Special Administration Region. Residents of Hong Kong throng by hydrofoil to Macau at weekends to pour into the casinos. Nevertheless, there is still enough left of old Macau to discover: the Portuguese-inspired façades, narrow alleys, markets and the pious offerings in Macau's temples.

Nuts and dried fruits at the bazar at Kashgar in western China on the old Silk Road. Above: Fishmongers in the streets of Kowloon, Hong Kong, tout their tempting wares straight from the sea. Right-hand page: dried fish and fresh seafood at a market in eastern China.

CHINESE CUISINE

Chinese cuisine is diverse indeed, reflecting the vast size of the country. Shark-fin soup, simple filled dumplings, formal banquets or street food: you name it, the quality is always good. Rice reigns supreme in the southern regions whereas wheat is king in the north. Four main culinary regions exemplify the range: Pekinese, Shanghai, Sichuan and Hunan cooking in the south-west and Cantonese in the south. Steamed buns and dumplings are everyday fare in the north, with delectable Peking Duck for special occasions. In Mongolia, meat and vegetables are cooked together over hot stones; Mongolian barbecue is a Western adaptation but hot pot is authentic. The cuisine of the Yangtze delta is famed for seafood and sweet-and-sour pork is also from this region. In the provinces of Sichuan and Hunan, food is hot and spicy and soya sauce is liberally used. Sichuan cooking features Sichuan peppercorns, ginger and herbs while chili peppers are used in many Hunan dishes, with orange chicken and crispy duck regional specialities. Cantonese cuisine is considered the most sophisticated in China. Fresh ingredients are key here. Suckling pig is a delicacy and the range of seafood is broad: oysters, unusual fish and shellfish. Chopsticks are used throughout China as eating utensils and meals consist of many courses, enjoyed in good company.

Wuzhizhou is one of the most beautiful islands in the Hainan Archipelago. The crystalline water is an Eldorado for scuba divers and fishermen. Above: Yalong Bay. This national resort has one of Hainan's most beautiful beaches. Below left: Coconut palms on the beaches of Hainan, rocky headlands and coral reefs on the Xisha Islands and in Qizhi Bay on Hainan.

Hainan

The Chinese used to regard the island of Hainan as the southern fringe of the known world. Imperial officials in disapproval were once exiled to languish on Hainan but the island is now an accessible Special Economic Zone in the Gulf of Tonking enjoying numerous benefits and a good tourism infrastructure. A tropical climate, dazzling white beaches, palms and evergreen-forested hills have made the island a popular destination with affluent Chinese from the north. With its luxury hotels and extensive resort facilities, Hainan is often compared to Hawaii although it has managed to keep its individual character for 2,000 years. Resident ethnic minorities make for a multicultural ambience. Hainan cuisine is richly varied, featuring fresh seafood, abundant vegetables and superb fruit. Add in lively markets and brightly temples and it is clear why this is a popular holiday region.

Large picture: In spite of the Cultural Revolution and communist ideology, religion is deeply rooted in the everyday lives of many Chinese. Here, offerings are presented in the Buddhist Wenshu Monastery in Chengdu. Above: The Three Pagodas of Chong Sheng Temple are near Dali Old Town. Built between AD 822 and AD 859, they exemplify the distinctive architectural style peculiar to the Bai people.

SOUTH-WESTERN CHINA

Sichuan, the province with the largest population (about 100 million) is called "China's Rice Bowl". Situated at the center of China, Sichuan Province is bounded in the west by the Tibetan high plateau and in the east by the great Yangtze River. The heart of the province is the Sichuan or "Red Basin", an agricultural cornucopia. Yunnan is in the south, bordering on Myanmar, Vietnam and Laos, at the confluence of three of Asia's greatest rivers. Yunnan is famed far beyond its borders for its superb teas and delicious fruit.

The Jiuzhaigou Valley boasts some of China's most beautiful natural scenery, with glassy lakes and primeval forests. Above: These terraces of calcite pools linked by waterfalls make the lake country of Huanglong spectacular. Below: Autumnal woods along the Shuzheng Lakes.

Jiuzhaigou and Huanglong

Jiuzhaigou Valley, which means the "Valley of Nine Villages", in northern Sichuan Province boasts magnificent unspoilt scenery in a high valley, where the picturesque villages after which the valley is named were populated by Tibetans. Here, lakes and ponds, multi-level waterfalls, limestone caverns, mixed forests and steep mountains, many of them snow-capped, radiate an unusual harmony in a primeval landscape. Jiuzhaigou is an unspoilt gem of nature. The coniferous and deciduous forests and the many rare, often endangered fauna species make this a natural botanical and zoological garden. Huanglong, "Yellow Dragon Gully", is famed for its magical golden calcite deposits in myriads of little lakes. Various species of aquatic flora tint the spectacular waters of Five Colour Pond so that it glows in five vibrant tones.

The Giant Panda, which is mainly herbivorous, feeding on bamboo shoots. Above: Bamboo forests are the Giant Panda's natural habitat. Below: Until recently, the Giant Panda was thought to be solitary, rarely meeting other members of its species. It can survive very cold winters.

THE GIANT PANDA

The Giant Panda is a living treasure in China and the emblem of the World Wide Fund for Nature. It is probably the best known endangered animal species. Giant Pandas live in six, small strictly protected areas in the provinces of Sichuan and Yunnan. In its homeland, supernatural powers are attributed to the Giant Panda:

it is said to ward off natural disasters and evil spirits. Written records mentioning the Giant Panda go back three thousand years. Chinese emperors kept Giant Pandas as pets. The Giant Panda's diet consists mainly of young bamboo shoots. Since bamboo is not very nourishing, a Giant Panda must eat vast quantities of it daily, which is why

it needs such an extensive habitat. This in turn leads to conflicts with local farmers. Otherwise the Giant Panda does not have many natural enemies. Until very recently, it was believed that the Giant Panda was solitary, paying little attention to other members of its species except in the mating season. Its dwindling habitat repre-

sents a major threat to the Giant Panda. Estimates of the number of Giant Pandas living in the wild range from about 1,400 to 3,000. Giant Pandas love the cool, damp climate of dense evergreen forests but one of the two species can live on snowy mountains above the tree line. Giant Pandas rarely reproduce in zoos.

Mount Emei is located about 150 km (93 miles) south-west of Chengdu. With its Golden Summit (Jinding Si) it is one of China's most sacred mountains. A plateau provides an impressive setting for a Buddhistic monastery. Above: Anlan Bridge on the Dujian embankment across the Min. Right-hand page: A temple in Du Jiang Yan, temple figures and a bridgewalk with red paper lanterns in Chengdu.

Chengdu and Dujiangyan

Chengdu is a modern urban metropolis (population 3.2 million) but visitors find it more like a quiet provincial city. Life is tranquil, the teahouses are packed and the markets overflown with local market-garden produce. The sprawling Wenshu Yuan temple complex and the garden around the hut once lived in by the Confucian poet Fu are well worth visiting. The Giant Panda Breeding and Research Centre, full of endearing baby pandas bred in captivity through scientific intervention, is only a few miles away. After two hours of driving west, the Du Jiang Yan irrigation system, featuring a still functional embankment built in 256 BC, divides the Min River, irrigates the Chengdu plain and deposits fertile silt on the fields. This marvel of ancient Chinese engineering has proved its worth down through the ages as protection against flooding at high water, which occurs frequently.

From a stairway, one can view the Giant Buddha Statue of Le-shan from various perspectives. Although it was restored in recent years, the over 700-year-old figure with its hands resting on its knees is suffering from erosion due to acid rain. Above: Carved into the cliff face of the Lingyun Mountain Range, the statue is to be found on a peninsula at the confluence of the Min, Dadu and Qingyi Rivers. Right-hand page: The Buddha statue is colossal: the head is 14 m (15 yds) high, the shoulders are 28 m (31 yds) across and the height of the figure is 71 m (78 yds).

Leshan

Surrounded by three rivers, Leshan looks back on three millennia of history. At the confluence of the Min, Dadu and Qingyi Rivers, one can find the world's largest seated Buddha statue, which even dwarfed the destroyed Buddha statues in Afghanistan. A monk began to carve this huge statue from the rock in the eighth century AD and it was completed ninety years later by his disciples. The figure is barefoot, with pendulous ear lobes and a tuft of hair twisted up in a spiral. Several miles across from it to the west, rises Mount Emei, one of the Four Sacred Mountains, from which Buddhism is said to have spread across China. At the foot of the mountain stands Baoguo Temple, with a copper-clad tower in fourteen tiers housing a precious porcelain Buddha. The Leshan Giant Buddha and the temple complex are part of the Mount Emei Scenic Area, a UNESCO Cultural World Heritage Site.

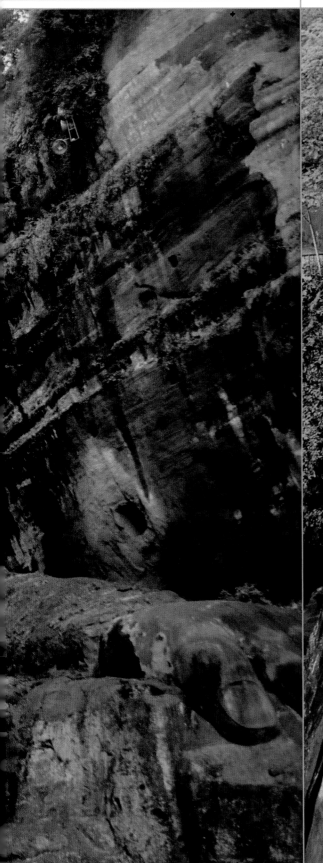

Between bright prayer flags lies the Buddhist cloister of Songzanlin. The building is similiar to the Potala Palace in Lhasa, the cloister is decorated with wood carvings and vivid tiles. It was built at the time of the fifth Dalai Lama about 300 years ago and houses valuable relics. Above: At Shigu, the Yangtze bends dramatically to form a loop before flowing north.

Zhongdian and Three Parallel Rivers National Park

"A paradise in the mountains, where people grow very old, enjoy learning, find inner peace and discover the meaning of all being that lies somewhere in Asia", is a general description of Shangri-La, the Lost Horizon for which many have yearned. The Chinese sought a place like that and found Zhongdian in a natural setting that is still unspoilt. North of Zhongdian, Songzanlin, a fully restored Tibetan cloister, nestles at the foot of a mountain. Snow-covered mountains up to 6,000 m (19,685 ft) high soar above the Yunnan landscape in which the three great rivers of Asia, the Salween, the Mekong and the Yangtze flow south in parallel courses. The rivers have gouged deep gorges into the countryside. The best known is narrow Hutiao Xia, "Tiger Leaping Gorge", named to commemorate a valiant tiger said to have leapt across the raging Yangtze.

The five arches of the bridge on Black Dragon Pool in Lijiang. Above: The Jade Dragon Bridge over the old city canal in old Lijiang and a wall painting in Dabaoji Palace. Below left: Red lanterns adorning a pagoda and a Nakhi woman in traditional costume looking in the mirror.

Lijiang

Lijiang is popular with visitors. Set in an enchanting landscape, it has a mild climate and the old town is romantic. This is the home of the Nakhi (Naxi) people, who are of Tibetan descent and still adhere to shamanistic beliefs. Crisscrossed by narrow canals, Lijiang has cobbled streets and venerable houses of wood and mudbrick surrounded by high walls. This is one of the best-preserved old towns in China. Sifang Square marks the center of the city, lined with small shops where Nakhi women dressed in traditional costume make their purchases. The women rule the household, taking all decisions, working in the fields and holding the purse-strings. The men, however, own the houses and land. The Nakhis have succeeded in preserving their cultural heritage, including their distinctive orchestral music and their own scripts, down through the centuries.

The Three Pagodas of Dali form an isoceles triangle. They have survived many severe earthquakes. Above: The Earth Forest in Yuanmou was formed two million years ago. Fantastically shaped, these tall pillars of stone are more than 40 m (44 yds) high.

Dali and the Earth Forest

Dali Old Town is situated at the foot of Cangshan. It is surrounded by high walls with fortified gates, of which only two have survived. The town is laid out like a chess-board and the streets are paved with flagstone. The roofs of the stone houses which line the streets have blue titles. Mountain streams flow through the alleys on their way north to the green waters of Lake Erhai with its three islands. The Three Pagodas of Chong Sheng Temple near the Old Town are the city landmark. The highest of the three pagodas boasts sixteen tiers of eaves adorned with Buddha statues. In northern Yunnan, plate tectonics movements and soil erosion two million years ago created the bizarre rock formations known as the Earth Forest. These grotesque marvels of nature recalling forms in El Greco or Cézanne elicit associations of forests, human bodies or even pagoda architecture.

Around 270 million years ago, a smooth sea in a karst mountain region developed into what we now call the "Stone Forest". The precipitous rock formations are accessible via walkways. These spectacular rocks often resemble animals or people and have been given interesting names such as "Birds feed their young" or "Preening phoenix". From a viewing pagoda one can have a look over the whole area. Above: The city of Kunming also has a few sites worth seeing such as the Jinma and the Biji Gate in the Jinbi Street or the Yuan Temple.

Kunming and the Stone Forest

A temperate climate and lovely verdant scenery have earned Kunming the accolade "Spring City". Surrounded on three sides by mountains, Kunming is bounded on the south by Lake Dian. Kunming (population about one million, including twelve ethnic minorities) is the political and cultural hub of the south-west. The Buddhist Yuantong Temple, the city's largest, has attracted pilgrims for some 1,200 years. The incredible Stone Forest, 120 km (74 miles) south of Kunming, is a karst landscape covering some 100 km (62 miles) that has been eroded over aeons of time into eerily beautiful rock formations, including spectacular subterranean phenomena and even a long lake with an underwater stone forest. Above ground, lofty cliffs and bizarre peaks have been weathered into forms resembling plants, animals and people: an inspiration to Chinese poets.

Yuanjiang is famed for its rice terraces. This landscape is at its verdant best in spring when the rice fields are under irrigation. Above: Waterfalls covering 4 km (2 miles) and 500 m (547 yds) across often plunge with a menacing roar into the depths of the Jiulong but in places trickle softly over calcite terraces. This place is one of the most popular sights to see in China. Below: The rice fields stretching flat across the plain at Luopingbur are laid out in hillside terraces in mountainous terrain.

Yuanjiang, Qiubei, De Tian and Jiulong

Yuanyang is accessible via a narrow road running through the Yuanjiang Gorge of the Yuang (Red River). The city near the river is set in a lush tropical arable landscape, where bananas, sugarcane and pineapples are grown. This region is also known for its quilt of terraced rice fields swirling over the hills. Quiubei and Puzhehei National Park are in south-eastern Yunnan, another spectacular karst landscape with caves, water-falls and crystalline lakes. Further south on the Vietnamese border, the De Tian Waterfall plunges with enormous force in three cascades 200 m (219 yds) wide. Near Luoping, west of Kunming, the grand Jiulong Waterfall accompanies the Jiulong River with ten cascades over a stretch of only 2 km (1 mile). The largest of these falls is Shenglong Waterfall, which is 56 m (61 yds) high and 110 m (120 yds) wide.

Since 1852, it has been common knowledge that Mount Everest, all 8,850 m (29,035 ft) of it, is the world's highest mountain. It straddles the border between Tibet and Nepal at the heart of the Himalayas (above). Prayer flags flutter in the breeze in front of Samye Monastery, which is situated about 100 km (62 miles) east of Lhasa. Samye was founded in the late eigth century AD.

WESTERN CHINA

Tibet, the mysterious plateau country in remote Central Asia has captured the European imagination perhaps more than any other country. Its borders are the highest mountain ranges on earth. Quiet landscapes of icy, snow-covered mountains, lakes and steppes are characteristic of Tibet. Its political status may be controversial but the Tibetan people are devoutly religious. To the north-east of Tibet is the Chinese province of Qinghai. This is a region of grassland and deserts, with a vast salt lake adding to its unique qualities.

The highest point of the Tangulla mountains is on the border from Qinghai to Tibet. The 6,559-m-high (21,519 ft) Geladaindong is also the source of the Jangtsekiang (Yangtze). Above: Snow fields on Mount Tanglha on the Qinghai-Tibet Highway. Below: The Lama monastery Longwu had been destroyed and has only recently been rebuilt. It houses numerous brigt paintings of gods and statues from Tibetan Buddhism. Below right: The Kumbum Monastery (known in Chinese as Ta'er Si) southwest of Xining is known for its yak-butter Buddha figures.

Remarkable cities and cultural monuments

▢ UNESCO World Heritage (Cultural)   ▲ Places of Buddhist cultural interest
▢ Remarkable cities   ▮ Castle/fortress/fort
⛩ Ancient China   ⛩ Tomb/grave
☪ Places of Islamic interest

MONGOLIA

Altayn Caadah Gov'

Gov'-Altay

Southern
Altay Gobi
Nature Reserve

Pd   Pe   141   Pf   Pg   Ph   Pj

86°   88°   90°   92°   94°   96°

Chaiwopu   Mori

Houxia   Dabancheng   Qijiaojing   Barkol Hu

Balguntay   Ulanlinggi   Toksum   Turpan   Bezeklik   Barkol   Nom
Qianfo Dong   Liaodun

Hejing   Hoxud   Jiaohe Gucheng   Astana   Shanshan   Yiwu
Argaybulak   Gaochang Gucheng
Daban   Aydingkol Hu

Yanqi   Kümüx   Turfan Depression   Hami   HMI   Atas Bogd

Korla   Bosten Hu   Hui Wangmu   Luotuoquanzi

Yuli   Hami   Yandun   Silk Road   Hongshishan
(Lop Nur)   Pendi

Qongkol   Aqitag   Weiya   Xingxingxia   Gongpo-
Gashun Gobi   quan

Mazong Shan

Tikanlik   Hongliuyuan

Loulan   Bai Shan
Gucheng

Lop Nur   Yumenguan   Anxi   Qiaowan

Ikanbujimal   Yumen Guan   Minghoshan   Yumen Zhen
Luobuzhuang   (Dunhuang)   DNH   Silk Road   Yumen
Mogao Ku   Yulinsi Shiku

Ruoqiang   Miran   Donglük   Yueya Quan
(Qarklik)   Yandaxkak   Baxkorgan   Silk Road   Aksay   Subei   Dalai Shan

Waxxari   Altun Shan   Dangjin Shankou   Jingtie Shan

Altun   Dingzikou   Jingtieshan

Mangnai Zhen   Lenghu   Huahaizi

Tomorlog   Huatugou   Tsagaan   Yema Nanshan
Chulunta

Youdunzi   Gebituolatuo   Shule Nanshan

Mangnai   Chalengkou   Yugia   Kangz'gyai
Iqe

Gansen   Har Hu

Xi Taijnar Hu   Da Qaidam

Dong Taijnar Hu   Bayan Shan

Urt Moron   Delhingha   Bugt Shan

Haya'er   Da Juh   Qarhan   Ga Hai   Ulan

Boluntay   Gashun-
chaka

Bukadaban   Golmud   Nomhon
Feng

GOQ   Balong   Dulan

Naij Tal   Xugui
Xiaonanchuan   Qagan Tahoi

Kunlun   Budongquan   Bacang
Shankou

Qumar Heyan   Gawa Obo
Yagradagzê
Shan

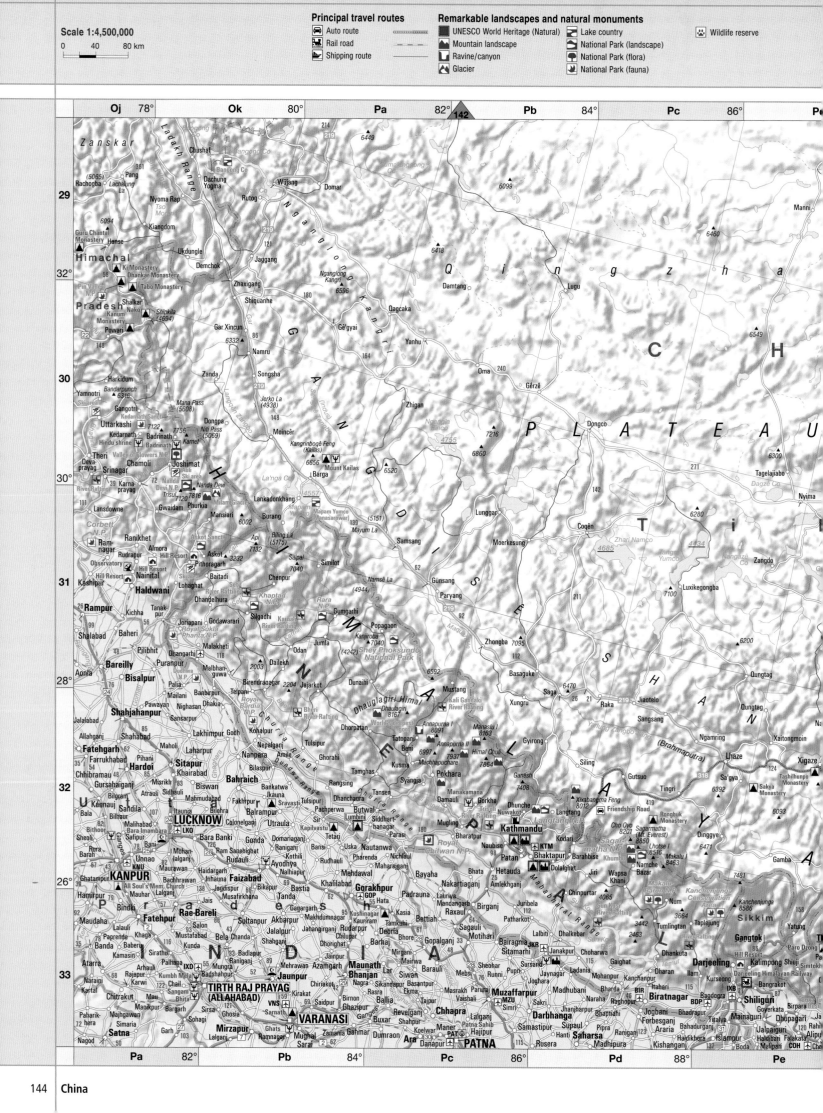

Principal travel routes

- Auto route
- Rail road
- Shipping route

Remarkable landscapes and natural monuments

- UNESCO World Heritage (Natural)
- Mountain landscape
- Ravine/canyon
- Glacier
- Lake country
- National Park (landscape)
- National Park (flora)
- National Park (fauna)
- Wildlife reserve

Remarkable cities and cultural monuments

☐ UNESCO World Heritage (Cultural)
☐ Remarkable cities
🏛 Ancient China
⛰ Places of Christian cultural interest

☪ Places of Islamic interest
▲ Places of Buddhist cultural interest
Ψ Places of Hindu cultural interest
Ψ Places of Sikh cultural interest

♜ Historical city scape
♜ Castle/fortress/fort
⌂ Palace
📡 Space telescope

🏛 Museum

Sport and leisure destinations

🎿 Skiing
🚣 Canoeing/rafting
⌂ Hill resort

Pe 90° Pf 92° Pg 143 94° Ph 96° Pj 98° Pk

KUNLUN SHAN

Gashun-chaka

Golmud
GOQ

Qaidam Pendi

2625

Qaidam He

4472 Ulan

128 109 Nomhon 53 109 4487
Xiaonanchuan Naij Tal 5390 Qagan Tahoi Burhan Budai Shan 151 3202 Dulan 27

Kunlun Shankou (4849) 6300 Budongquan 5123 Xugui 4491 Bacang 36°

Qumar Heyan 59 Gawa Obo

Xi sh a n Hoh Xil Hu
Huiten Nur
Xijir Ulan Hu
Ulan Ul Hu

Bukadaban Feng 6860

Dongai Coring 4814

G a o y u a n Qinghai

Qumar He 109 Yagradagzê Shan 5202 Bayan Har Shan Donggi Cona

Wuli Qiclou Huashixia 4285 Madoi Ngoring Hu Yamatan 28

Tuotuo Heyan Moron Us Tongtian He Tukola Tolha Bayan Har Shan 5267 Cairiwa

4746 Geladaindong 6559 167 Kulanhor Zhidoi Qumarlêb (5100) Bayan Har Shankou Horgorguinba 34°

Tanggula Shan 6241 Wequan Kili Bulak 338 Qingshuihe

I N A O F T I B E T

Tanggula Shankou (5160) 5776 Xiwu

5880 Zadoi Yushu Chumda Sêrxü

Bogcang He 109 82 Za Qu (Mekong) Toramarkog 138 Zogqên 29 147

Amdo Monza Nangqên Chola Shankou Maniganggo

e Co Doba 207 Dongqiao Nyainrong 116 Nangqên 6168 Chola Shan 32°

Baingoin 317 Xagquka 73 Boqên Gushi Dêgê 91 Lama Monastery Gamtog

89 Sog Xian 174 Serca Riwoqê Jomda (4633) 317 110 Baiyü Rasha

Namco 172 Nagqu Dênggên 86 Enda Qamdo Toba

4590 Nam Co Horra Kyogche La (4900) 117 Riwoqê 188 51

Dêqên NYAINQÊNTANGLHA SHAN Damxung Banbar Gyitang Radzi 171 214 30

Nyainqêntanglha 7114 Feng 64 Atlas Gompa Lhari Alamdo Lhorong Bamda 4907 Yidun

Yangbajain Tangmai Baxoi 5008 Batang

Margyang 75 Sera Monastery Maizhokunggar Jimda Bomi Zogang 158 Mongotong

Drepung Monastery Potala 318 Gongbogyamda 401 118 Sumzom 185 Gartog Chubalung

Nethang Temple 50 Jokhang Ganden Bayizhen Namjagbarwa 7755 225 318 Rawu 5119

Quxu Lhasa Rito Gompar Nyingchi 5966 Bruni Zongza

Rinbung LXA Gonggar Zhanang Samye Monastery Zétang Nang Xian Mainling Caka'lho 31

Friendship Road Gonggar Monastery 87 Qusum Miging 4255 Zhowagoin 232 Guihua Temple

Nagarze 160 Samzhou Yumco Qonggyai Gyaca Gyaca 4639 Tato Yiyu Karko 4157 Ilupu 4776

Daglung Samding Monastery 4432 Shol Mega Along Zazhong Mabating Dêqên

Puma Yumco Lhozhan 7554 Kulha Gangri Lhünzê 4812 Voring 3992 Kamberg Amili Nixi

Melunghi Gang Cona Kangto 7089 Sartam Daporijo Kombong Dambuk Nizamghat Hayuliang Walong Dong 5051 Zhongdian

7000 Thowada Goemba Tamshing Goemba Jang Se La 4249 Par Marniu Arunachal Pradesh Yanmen

BHUTAN Jakar Donkar Tawang Buddhist Monastery 3776 Tado Daring Sadiya Tezu Brakmakund 4578 Hkyenhpa Gongshan 4401

Black Mountain 4915 Trashigang Bomdi La Seppa Ziro Jonai Bazar DIB Chonkham Naung-Mon 32

Gangola Narphung 4523 Sachida Itanagar Pathalipam Bordoloni Brahmaputra Tinsukia Makum Tapun Miao Hpungan Pass MYANMAR (BURMA) Yatang

2219 Darranga Doimara Nameri N.P. Nij Lalyk Dibrugarh North Lakhimpur Dihajan Jaipur Margherita Namdapha N.P. 4022 (3072) 28°

Pf 92° Pg 94° Ph 96° Pj 98° Pk

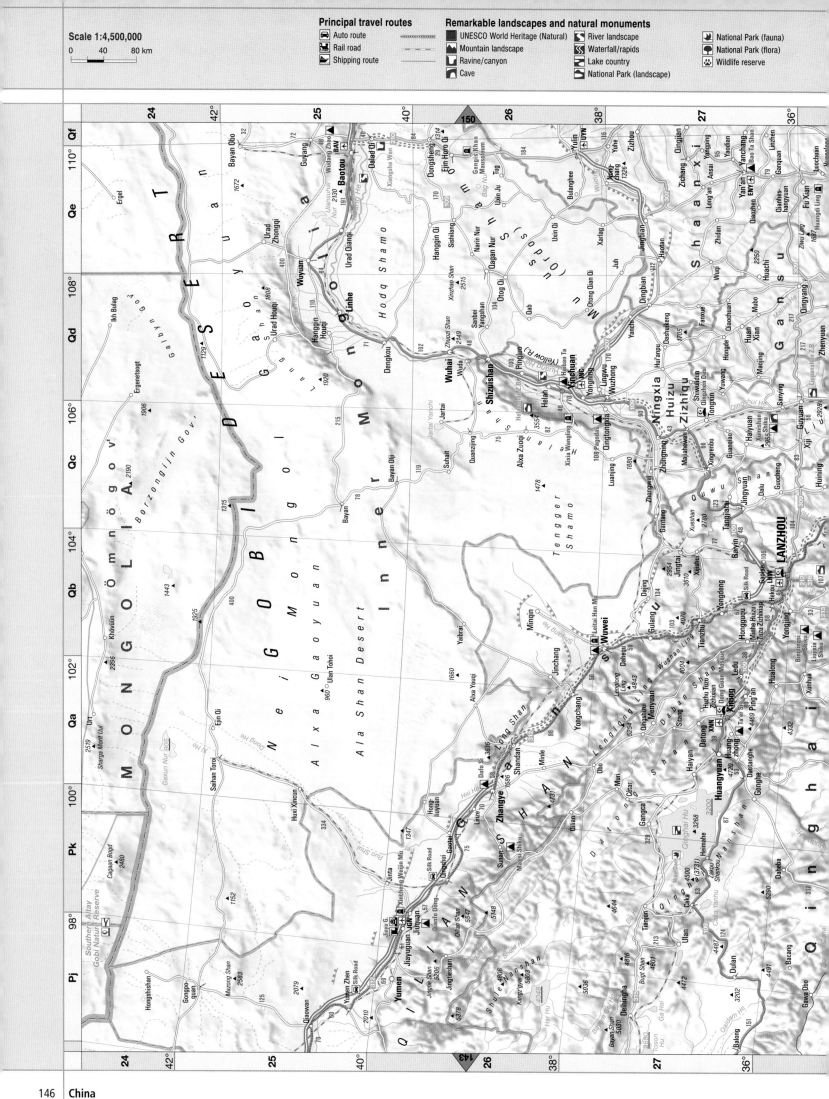

Remarkable cities and cultural monuments

- ☐ UNESCO World Heritage (Cultural)
- ☐ Remarkable cities
- ⚿ Ancient China
- ☪ Places of Islamic cultural interest
- ▲ Places of Buddhist cultural interest
- ∞ Cultural landscape
- ⚔ Castle/fortress/fort
- ⚰ Tomb/grave
- 🏛 Museum

Sport and leisure destinations

- ♨ Mineral/thermal spa
- ☺ Amusement/theme park

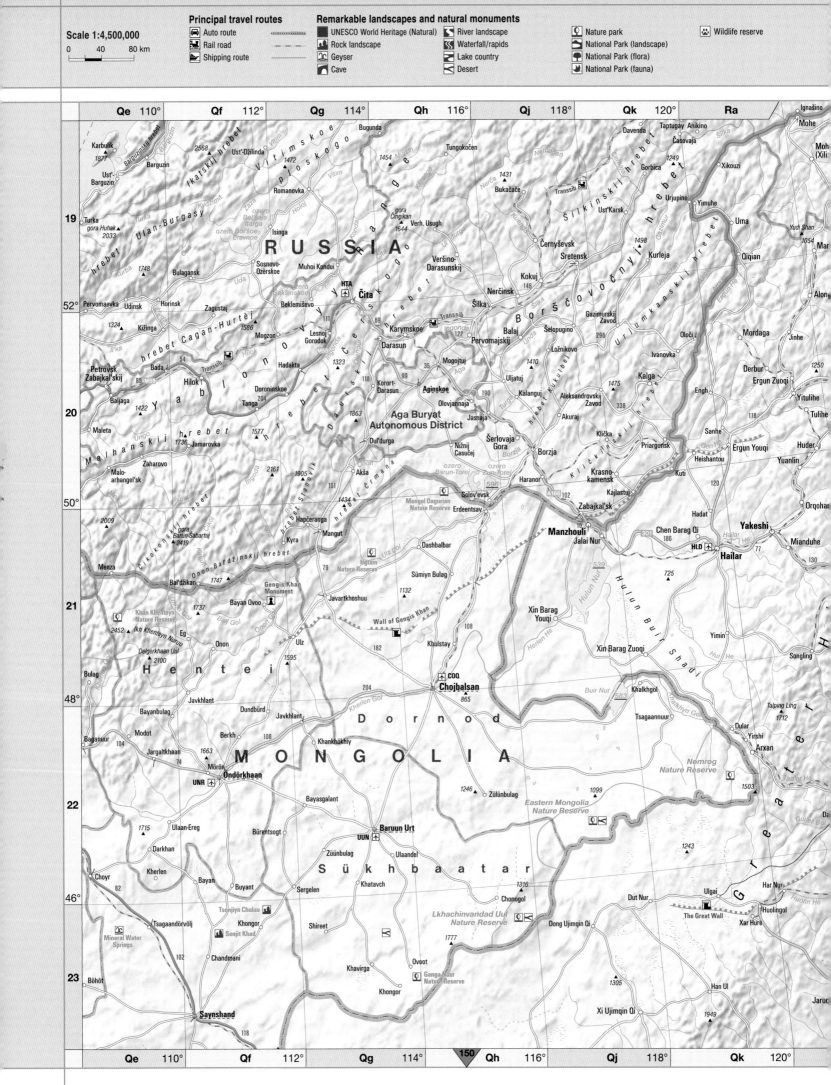

Scale 1:4,500,000

0   40   80 km

Principal travel routes

- Auto route
- Rail road
- Shipping route

Remarkable landscapes and natural monuments

- UNESCO World Heritage (Natural)
- Rock landscape
- Geyser
- Cave
- River landscape
- Waterfall/rapids
- Lake country
- Desert
- Nature park
- National Park (landscape)
- National Park (flora)
- National Park (fauna)
- Wildlife reserve

RUSSIA

MONGOLIA

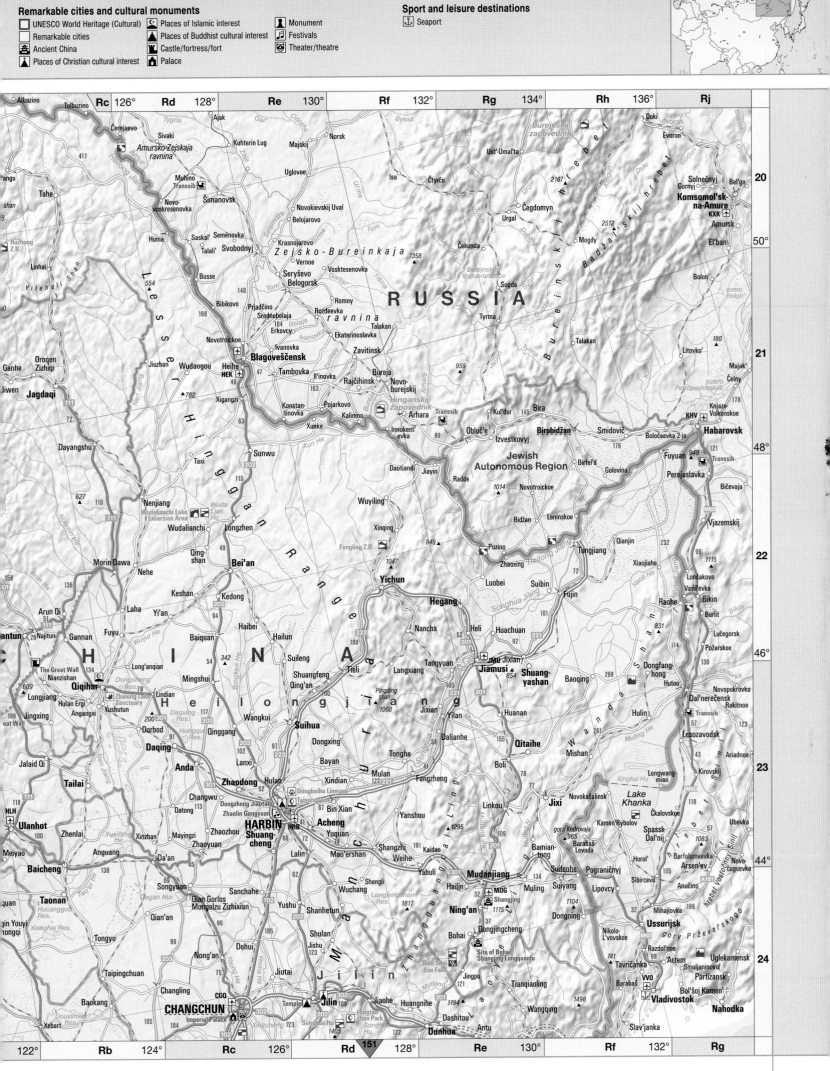

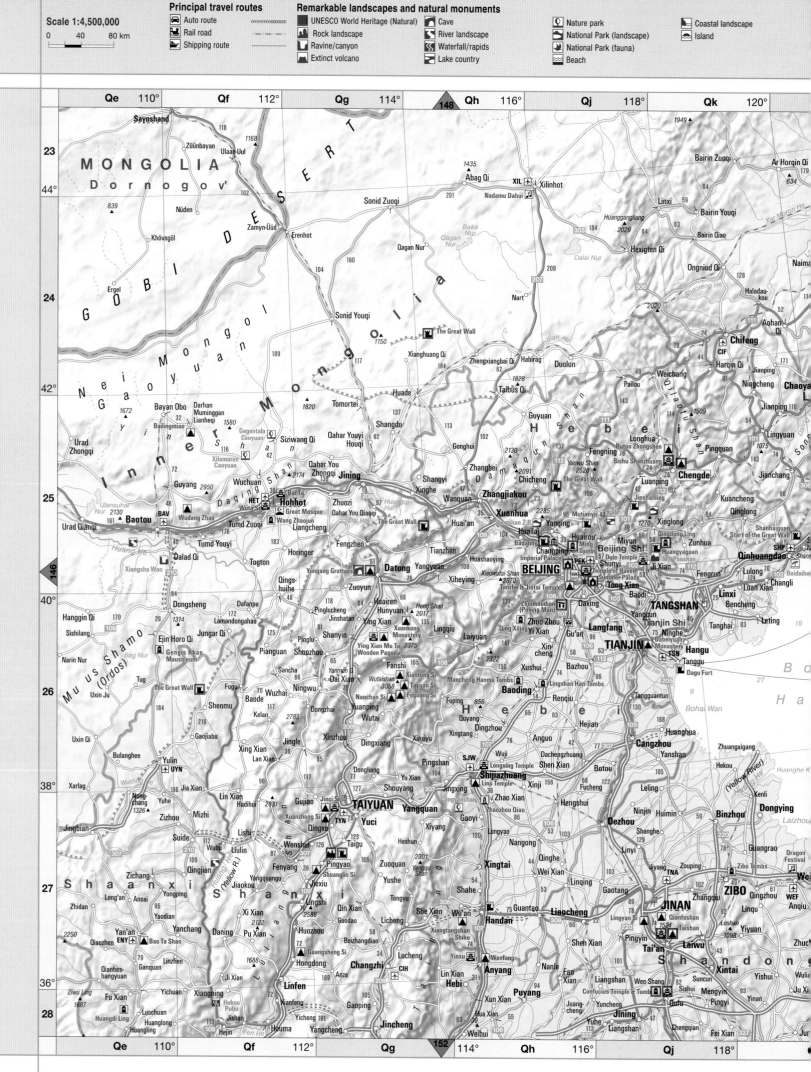

Principal travel routes

- Auto route
- Rail road
- Highspeed train
- Shipping route

Remarkable landscapes and natural monuments

- UNESCO World Heritage (Natural)
- Rock landscape
- Ravine/canyon
- Geyser
- Cave
- River landscape
- Waterfall/rapids
- Lake country
- Nature park
- National Park (landscape)
- National Park (flora)
- National Park (fauna)
- Coastal landscape

Remarkable cities and cultural monuments

☐ UNESCO World Heritage (Cultural)
☐ Remarkable cities
🏯 Ancient China
▲ Places of Buddhist cultural interest
🏛 Historical city scape
📶 Impressive skyline
🏰 Castle/fortress/fort
⬚ Dam
⛉ Remarkable bridge
⛩ Tomb/grave
✕ Theater/theatre of war
⛏ Market

Sport and leisure destinations

🏁 Race track
⚓ Seaport
♨ Mineral/thermal spa

Ra 122° Rb 124° 151 Rc 126° Rd 128° Re 130°

Hong Do
Tadohae
Haesang
N.P.
Chin Do Chindo
Wando
Chongsan
Do
Komun Do
Tadohae Haesang
National Park

SOUTH KOREA

Hajo Do
Po-kil Do

Sohuksan Do

Cheju Haehyop

Kuiwa

Cheju
CJU
Hallasan
1950
Sunke and Manjang Caverns
Hallasan N.P.

Cheju Do

Taejong
Soguip'o

Y e l l o w   S e a

Katsumoto
Iki IKI
Gonoura
Karatsu
Hirado
Uku-jima
Ojika-jima
Hirado-jima
Sasebo
Goto-
Nakadori-jima
Arikawa Nishi-
Sonogi-
hanto
Naru-jima
Narao
retto
Hisaka-jima
Fukue-jima
429 Fukue
Sakai N.P.
FUJ

JAPAN

29

32°

Danjo-gunto

696

30

Zhongxin
Gang
Xinchuan Gang
Bencha

Taowang Gang

29

Changjiang Kou

SHANGHAI

Shanghai Shi

Shengsi Liedao

Daqu Dao
Shanghai Deepwater Port

E A S T   C H I N A

1213

1028

31

73

106

850

S E A

28°

229

Tori-
jima

89

103

Iheya-jima
Iheya

Izena-jima

Ie-jima

Aguni-jima

790

Motobu
Nago
Ishikawa

Okinawa
OKA

Kume-jima

Naha

Gushikawa

Kerama-retto

Gyokusendo
(Cave)

26°

JAPAN

33

Sekibisho Jima

Uotsuri
Jima

Shenkaku Islands

Pengchia Yü

FUZHOU
FOC

Qk 120° Ra 156 122° Rb 124° Rc 126° Rd

China 153

UNESCO World Heritage (Cultural)   Ancient China   Cultural landscape   Tomb/grave   Sport and leisure destinations

Remarkable cities   Places of Christian cultural interest   Historical city scape   Theater/theatre of war   Horse racing

Pre- and early history   Places of Buddhist cultural interest   Impressive skyline   Museum   Seaport

Prehistoric rockscape   Pl. of cult. interest to indig. peoples   Remarkable bridge   Beach resort   Mineral/thermal spa

Principal travel routes
Auto route
Rail road
Shipping route

Remarkable landscapes and natural monuments
UNESCO World Heritage (Natural)
Mountain landscape
Rock landscape
Ravine/canyon
Cave
National Park (landscape)
National Park (flora)
Coastal landscape

Remarkable cities and cultural monuments
UNESCO World Heritage (Cultural)
Remarkable cities
Ancient China
Places of Christian cultural interest
Places of Buddhist cultural interest
Historical city scape
Impressive skyline
Museum

Scale 1:4,500,000

0   40   80 km

Qh 116°   Qj 118°   Qk 120°   Ra 122°   Rb 124°

Jinniu 67
Xianning 774
Wuxue
Konglong
Pengze 59
Huangshan
Xidi Hongcun
Chun'an
Mei-cheng
Pujiang
Xin-chang 73
Ninghai
Shipu
73

Yangxin
Matou 35
Hukou 24
Hongwei
Zhejiang
Jiande
Yiwu
Dongyang
Tiantai 149

Wenquanzhen
Tongshan
Ruichang
Jiujiang
Zhangjialing
Tian-bantie
JDZ 45
Jingdezhen
Wuyuan 56
Huabu
Longyou
Wuyi
Yongkang
Xianju 1382
Linhai
Qiansuo
Jiaojiang

De'an 81
Duchang 93
Jinhua
Shizu
Huangyan
Songmen

Wuning 65
Lushan 1474
Poyanghu Z.B.
Leping
Dexing
Chang-shan 1817
Quzhou
Jiang-shan 65
Suichang
Songyang
Lishui
Yantou
Wenling
Hongqiao 58

NANCHANG
NAO
Liantang
Xiangtang
Yugan
Wannian
Yongcheng
Jiulong Shan 1724
Xianxia Ling
Longquan 330
Qingtian
Yunhe
Yongjia
Wenzhou
WNZ

E A S T   C H I N A

Xiushui
Anyi
Yongxiu 105
J34
Boyang
Yiyang 65
Shangrao
Hekou
Yongping
Yingtan
Huangguang Shan 2165
Pucheng
Qingyuan
Dong-keng
Taishun
Nanyangdan Shan 1237
Pingyang
Rui'an
Aojiang

S E A

Tonggu
Jing'an
Shangfu
Fengxin
Xinjian
Jinxian
Dongxiang 60
Zhang-shu
Linchuan
Chongren
Nancheng
Guangze
Jianyang
Shuiji
Zhenghe
Zhouning
Fu'an
Fuding
Fanshan

Wumei Shan 1794
Daduan
Dacheng 64
Gao'an
Fengcheng
Yihuang
Nanfeng
Shaowu
Jian'ou
Pingnan
Huangsha
Xiapu
Sansha

Yifeng 320
Yongfeng
Le'an
Lichuan
Shunchang
Zhenqian
Zhouning
Lüxia
Funing Wan

Yichun 67
Xinyu
Yong-feng
Gonxi 76
Jianning
Taining
Jiangle
Jian'ou
Shun-chang
Huangsha
Ningde
25

Wudong Shan 1918
Anfu
Jishui
Jinggang-shan
Guangchang
Jianning
Jiangle
Nanping 96
Gutian
Luoyuan
Sansha Wan

Ji'an
Qingyuanshan
Taihe
Ningdu 123
Jinggang-shan
Ninghua
Sanming
Minqing 48
Bai Ta 54
Lianjiang
Matsu Lietao

Yongxin 81
Jinggangshan
Xingguo
Shicheng
Ninghua
Yong'an
Minqing
FUZHOU
FOC
Yong Quan Si
Gushan
Changle

KOW
Ganzhou 125 323
Yudu
Ruijin
Changting 84
Dehua
Xianyou
Putian
Longtian
Haitan Dao
Pingtan
Pengchia Yü
Huaping Yü

Chongyi
Nankang 17
Huichang
Pengkou
Zhangping
Hua'an
Qingyuanshan 118
Nanri Dao

Dayu
Xinfeng 43
Wuping
Shanghang
Yong-ding
Tong'an
Anhai
Meizhou Dao
Mazur Miao
Chongwu
Fukuei Chiao
Keelung
Fulung
Fulung Seaside Park

Xiaomei 60
Anyuan
Jiaoling
Longyan
Hua'an
Quanzhou
Qingling Mosque
Kaiyuan Temple
Long Shan S.
Yangmingshan N.P.
Taipei Financial Centre
TPE
Northeast Coast Nat. Scenic Area

Nanxiong
Longnan
Dingnan
Xunwu
Changtai
Jimei
Shishi
Weitou
Taoyuan
Taipei
TAIPEI

Shixing
Pingyuan
Xingning
Zhangzhou
Xiamen (Amoy)
XMN
Chinmen
Gulangyu
Nanputuo Si
Zhenhai
Hsinchu
Wulai
Window on China
Ilan
Suao

Heping
Lianping
Wuhua
Pinghe
Zhangpu
Miao Li
Fengyuan
Hsuen Shan 3931
Chilan
9

Xingfeng
Longchuan
Fengshun
Fenghuang
Yunxiao
Taroko N.P.
TXG
Taichung
Poli 245
Tayuling 3559
Taroko

Longmen
Heyuan 912
Zhongba
Zijin
Jieyang
Raoping
Changhua
Nantou
Sun Moon Lake
Yushan 3952
Hualien
Kuangfu
Fengpin

Pingling
Luofushan
Chaozhou
Jiexi
Luhe
Chenghai
Nan'ao Dao
Yuanlin 112
Taishi
Lukang Folk Arts Festival
Aishan
Yu Shan
Pahsien Cave

Guangdong
Yancun 76
Siqu
Puning
Chadyan
Shantou
SWA
Nanpeng Liedao
Lukang
Matsu Temple
Chiayi
CYI
Ali-shan N.P.
Yuli
Changpin

Xinzuotang
Feng'an 1336
Jieshi
Huilai
Tropic of Cancer
Paisha
Waian
Putai
Hsinying 210
Taiwan

Huizhou
HUZ
Haifeng
Shanwei
Jieshi Wan
Penghu Islands (Pescadores)
Fort Zeelanda
Ta Yü
Tainan
TNN
TTT
Taitung
Lutao (Green I.)
Saltwater Hot Springs

Huidong
Lufeng
Zhelang
Taiwan Bank
Buddha Mountain
Dragon and Tiger Pagodas
Pingtung
Fengshan
Chiphen Hot Springs

SZX
Shenzhen
Disneyland
Kowloon (Jiulong)
KHH
KAOHSIUNG
Fangliao 65 98
Liuchiu Yü
Tajen
Lanyu

HKG
Happy Valley/Sha Tin
HONG KONG
Hong Kong/Xianggang
Fanglong
Checheng 40
Chihsing Yen
Hengchun
Oluanpi
Kenting N.P.
Lanyu

Lantau
Dangan Liedao
Wanshan Qundao

S O U T H   C H I N A

Luzon Strait

26

Itbayat
Itbayat I.
Batan Islands
Basco
Batan I.

Dongsha Qundao

S E A
386

Uyugan
Sabidug
Sabtang I.
Balintang I.

PHILIPPINES
Babuyan I.
San Dionisio

Balintang Channel